THE
EIGHT
WONDROUS
MINDS

Wholesome Vision

The Eight Wondrous Minds
Publisher: Wholesome Vision ©
Author: Chen Yi Sheng Zi (陳禕勝子)
Illustrations: Cover, p.1, 3, 4, 18, 23,
24, 27, © Shutterstock.com
1405 Bodega Way #5 Diamond Bar
CA 91765, USA
Tel: 1-909-638-7179
Fax: 1-626-839-5333
Website of Wholesome Vision:
WholesomeVision.com

ISBN (ebook): 978-1-945892-07-3
First U.S. Edition

How many minds do we have?
We usually think of ourselves as having one
single mind. Psychologists, neurologists and
philosophers have classified the human mind
into different domains or levels such as the
conscious and subconscious. Buddhism
suggests another understanding of mind.

According to the teachings of Buddha Shakyamuni, every one of us has eight distinct minds. In Buddhist scriptures, these eight minds are usually called the "eight consciousnesses," with the word "consciousness" defined as the function of awareness and discernment.

The eye-consciousness, our sight,
detects and differentiates colors
and visual objects.
The ear-consciousness, our hearing,
detects and differentiates sounds.
The nose-consciousness, our smell,
detects and differentiates odors.
The tongue-consciousness, our taste,
detects and differentiates flavors.
The body-consciousness, our touch,
detects and differentiates
physical sensations.

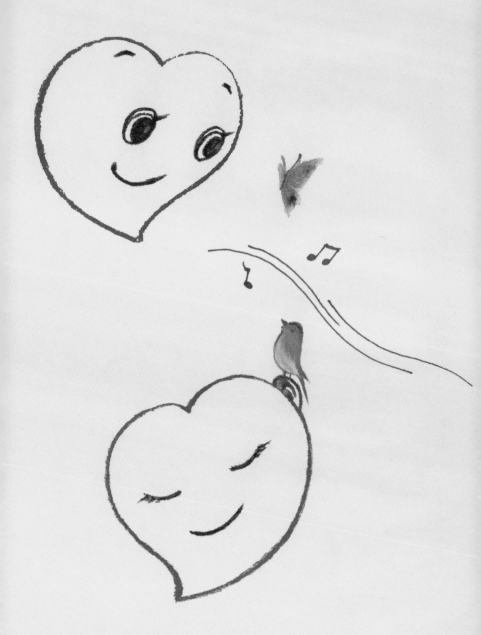

The sixth consciousness is the mental consciousness, or what we usually think of as the mind. The mental consciousness has a variety of functions, such as deliberation, memorization, analysis, inference, and abstract thinking. It can also receive and analyze all the information collected by the five sense consciousnesses.

Most of us have not heard of the seventh consciousness. In Buddhist scriptures, it's called the manas-consciousness. The manas-consciousness is quite special because it makes decisions and gives orders. In everyday life, for instance, it is this mind that decides one should go to bed, take a walk, eat, wash, etc. But since the way it works is rather subtle, we usually are unaware of its presence.

The eighth consciousness is the most special and enigmatic. It is known in Buddhism as the ālaya-consciousness, the foundational consciousness, or the Buddha-Essence. It is like a powerful video recorder that can keep account of every little thing we do. We are totally oblivious to its existence, yet it is the foundational mind-entity of our being.

In summary, the first six consciousnesses perceive and distinguish what is going on around us. The seventh consciousness decides and gives orders regarding everything at all times. The eighth consciousness impartially records and stores an individual's every single action.

If the body and mind were thought of as a huge corporation, these eight consciousnesses would be sort of like the CEO, general manager, supervisor, and receptionists and staffs who run its operation. If they do not work together in perfect harmony, we cannot live a normal life in this world.

Before Buddha Shakyamuni appeared in this world, humans were not aware that they have eight consciousnesses. The general public and most religions believe that our thinking mind — the mental consciousness is our soul, and it can continue to exist and move on to take a new form of existence after we die.

But the Buddha made it clear in his teachings that the mental consciousness is not eternal. It disappears when we fall asleep and cannot move on to future lives. Among the eight consciousnesses, only the eighth consciousness, the Buddha-Essence, can exist forever. It will impartially and accurately manifest the form of existence we should take in the next life according to our karmic records; simply speaking, a virtuous person who performs wholesome deeds will be reborn in a pleasurable environment, a person who performs unwholesome deeds will have to suffer the painful consequences of his or her bad deeds, such as being reborn as an animal in a future life.

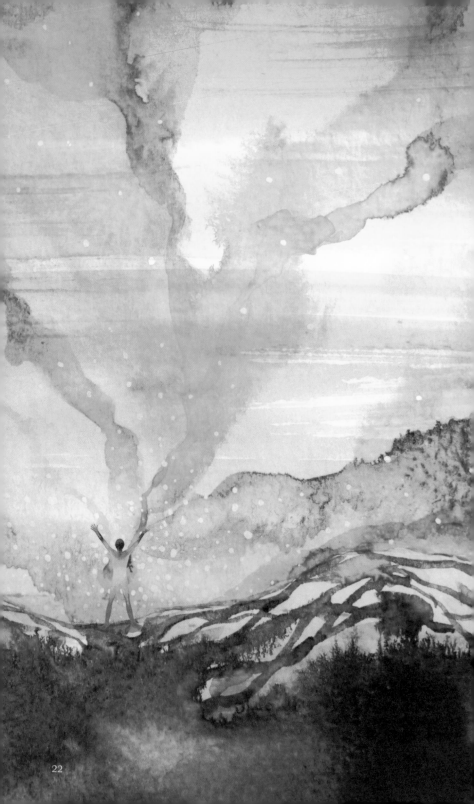

In fact, every one of us has our own Buddha-Essence that creates our body and mind. Not just humans, any sentient being, even one as tiny as an ant, has its own Buddha-Essence. As for the physical world—the mountains, landmasses, oceans, planets, galaxies, and even the entire universe—it is created collectively by the Buddha-Essence of karmically-related sentient beings. You may think of the Buddha-Essence as an invisible magician.

Why should we care about the existence of these eight consciousnesses and what they do? By knowing how these eight consciousnesses work together, we would be able to thoroughly and permanently clear away negative emotions and habitual tendencies, increase mental concentration, make better judgments, and so forth. As a result, we can live a happier and more fulfilling life with wisdom and freedom.

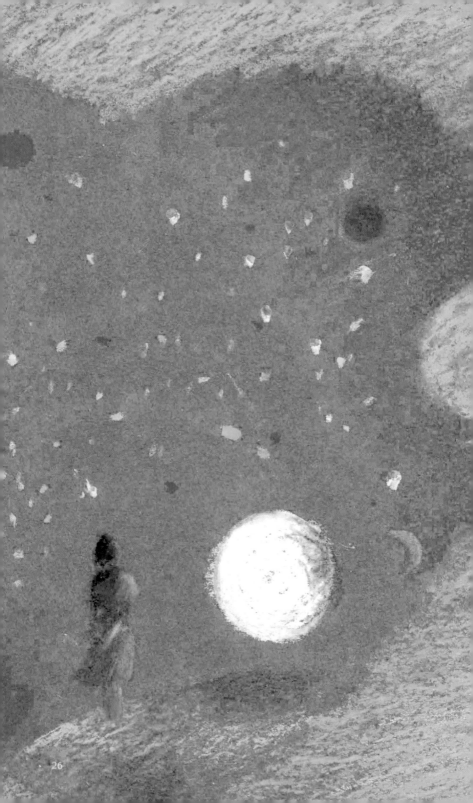

The Buddha taught us about the Buddha-Essence because he wanted us to understand the ultimate reality of our existence so that we can free ourselves from miseries and suffering. When we have found the Buddha-Essence, we can gradually unlock the miraculous power it possesses. Eventually, we can even acquire omniscience — the complete and perfect enlightenment of a Buddha, and we will be able to take full control of our lives just like the Buddha.

Following is a witty poem that
sums up the characteristics of these
eight consciousnesses:

Eight brothers live under one roof:
One is sharp, one is dim,
five do business out front,
and the last one keeps
tabs on everything.

POSTSCRIPT

Written based on Xuanzang's doctrinal expositions, this book is meant to introduce to the readers the Buddhist doctrine of eight consciousnesses. Among the eight consciousnesses, the eighth (ālaya) consciousness is the central and foundational Buddhist tenet and the permanent true mind Buddhist disciples seek awakening to. In Buddhist scriptures, it is also called the maturational consciousness (vipākavijñāna), the immaculate consciousness (amalavijñāna), and the tathāgatagarbha. Chan Buddhism alludes to it as one's original face before birth, one's native scenery, no-mind (the mind that does not see, hear, feel or know), the true mind, the diamond mind, Buddha, Dharma, the Mo Xie blade, and so forth.

Xuanzang, one of the most illustrious Buddhist masters in Chinese history, attained awakening to the eighth consciousness (tathāgatagarbha) in his teens. In order to learn about the post-awakening cultivation stages toward Buddhahood, he took a perilous journey to India to seek the original scriptures that shed light on this subject. One of the key Sanskrit texts he sought was the *Treatise on the Stages of Yogic Practice* (Yogācārabhūmiśāstra; a.k.a. *Treatise on the Seventeen Stages*). During his stay in India, King Harsha invited Xuanzang to host a public religious debate. With his remarkable eloquence, Xuanzang won the debate and made his name known throughout the five Indian kingdoms. He

was honored as the "deity of liberation" and the "deity of Mahayana Ultimate Truth" by Buddhists and heretics alike. Having acquired penetrative insights into Buddhist doctrines, Xuanzang translated an enormous amount of Sanskrit scriptures into Chinese after his return to China and authored the *Treatise on the Establishment of Consciousness-Only* and *Verses Delineating the Eight Consciousnesses* to articulate the self-nature of the eight consciousnesses. His profound and eloquent expositions continue to be read with admiration to this day.

Xuanzang was not the only practitioner in Chinese Buddhist history to have awakened to the eighth consciousness. The patriarchs of Chinese Chan tradition also attained the same awakening. Bodhidharma affirmed the second Chan patriarch Huike's awakening to the eighth consciousness with the *Lankāvatāra Sūtra*. The fifth patriarch Hongren verified the sixth patriarch Huineng's awakening to the eighth consciousness with the *Diamond Sūtra*, upon which Huineng exclaimed:

> Who could have thought that the self-nature is intrinsically uncreated and unceasing! Who could have thought that the self-nature can give rise to all phenomena!

In the Song Dynasty, Chan masters Dahui Zonggao and Hongzhi Zhengjue began to teach the Dharma after attaining direct realization of the eighth consciousness. They respectively advocated the method of *kanhua Chan* (Chan of meditation on critical phrase) and *mozhao Chan* (Chan of silent illumination). The two masters became lifelong friends because of having achieved awakening to the eighth consciousness.

In Tibet the two great masters of the Jonang tradition, Dölpopa Shérap Gyeltsen and Tāranātha, also attained awakening to the eighth consciousness. Based upon their realizations, Dölpopa expounded the doctrine of "other-emptiness" in his influential exposition *Mountain Doctrine* while Tāranātha discoursed on the same subject in his work *Essence of Other-Emptiness*, among many others.

In contrast to the uncreated and unceasing eighth consciousness, the mental consciousness is a phenomenon with origination and cessation—it will cease during deep sleep, fainting, the absorption of nonperception, the absorption of cessation, and complete death. It does not come from a previous life and cannot persist to future lives. The sixth (mental) consciousness can only arise from the eighth consciousness in dependence on two necessary conditions: the mental faculty (manas-consciousness) and the mental objects. These properties of the mental consciousness were affirmed by Buddha Shakyamuni and can be directly perceived by all enlightened persons.

Moreover, the thoughtless and numinous awareness attained during sitting meditation is a state of the mental consciousness, regardless of whether the five sense objects are present in this mental state or not. Even in the absence of the five sense objects, the thoughtless and numinous awareness attained in the second dhyāna through to the absorption of neither perception nor nonperception is still within the confines of the mental consciousness. Likewise, the union of bliss and emptiness realized during the sexual yoga practiced by Tibetan lamas is also a state of the mental consciousness. Beyond the fact that the mental consciousness itself can only arise from the eighth consciousness in dependence on the mental faculty (manasconsciousness) and the mental objects, the mental faculty and the mental objects themselves also arise from the seemingly dim and unresponsive eighth consciousness. After their arising, the mental consciousness, mental faculty, and mental objects continue to rely on the eighth consciousness to sustain their continued existence and operation.

In short, the mind that Buddhist practitioners seek awakening to is the eighth consciousness, not the mental consciousness. For this reason, those who refute the doctrine of eight consciousnesses, and believe only in the existence of six consciousnesses, can never achieve enlightenment within the Three Vehicles of Buddhist cultivation.

CULTIVATION CENTERS OF THE TRUE ENLIGHTENMENT PRACTITIONERS ASSOCIATION

Taipei Headquarters: 9F, No. 277, Sec. 3, Chengde Rd., Taipei 103, Taiwan. Tel.: +886-2-2595-7295 Ext. 10 & II for 9F; 15 & 16 for 10F; 18 & 19 for 5F; and 14 for the bookstore on 10F.)

Daxi Patriarch Hall: No. 5-6, Kengdi, Ln. 650, Xinyi Rd., Daxi Township,Taoyuan County 335, Taiwan.
Tel.: +886-3-388-6110

Taoyuan Lecture Hall: 10F, No. 286 & 288,Jieshou Rd., Taoyuan 330, Taiwan. Tel.: +886-3-374-9363

Hsinchu Lecture Hall: 2F-1, No. 55, Dongguang Rd., Hsinchu 300, Taiwan. Tel.: +886-3-572-4297

Taichung Lecture Hall: 13F -4, No. 666, Sec. 2, Wuquan W. Rd., Nantun Dist., Taichung 408, Taiwan.
Tel.: +886-4-2381-6090

Jiayi Lecture Hall: 8F-1, No. 288, Youai Rd., Jiayi 600, Taiwan. Tel.: +886-5-231-8228

Tainan Lecture Hall: 4F, No. 15, Sec. 4, Ximen Rd., Tainan 700, Taiwan. Tel.: +886-6-282-0541

Kaohsiung Lecture Hall: 5F, No. 45, Zhongzheng 3rd Rd., Kaohsiung 800, Taiwan. Tel.: +886-7-223-4248

Los Angeles Lecture Hall: 825 S. Lemon Ave, Diamond Bar, CA 91789, U.S.A. Tel.: +1-909-595-1-626-454-0607

Hong Kong Lecture Hall: Unit E, 27th Floor, TG Place, 10 Shing Yip Street, Kwun Tong, Kowloon, Hong Kong.
Tel: +852-2326-2231

Readers may download free publications of the Association from the website of True Wisdom Publishing Center:
http://books.enlighten.org.tw

八個奇妙的心

一個人究竟有幾個心？心理學家、腦神經醫師和哲學家的說法不一，但是他們都把人類的心靈和心智劃分為不同的區域和層次。

您可知道釋迦牟尼佛是怎麼說的嗎？

43

根據釋迦牟尼佛的教導，我們每個人都有八個心。在佛經裡，這八個心通常被稱為「八識」，「識」是指能夠認知的功能。

眼識就是我們的視覺功能，
感知和分辨色彩和影像。
耳識就是我們的聽覺，感知和分辨聲音。
鼻識就是我們的嗅覺，感知和分辨氣味。
舌識就是我們的味覺，感知和分辨味道。
身識就是我們的觸覺，感知和分辨身體
的各種感覺，譬如冷熱痛癢。

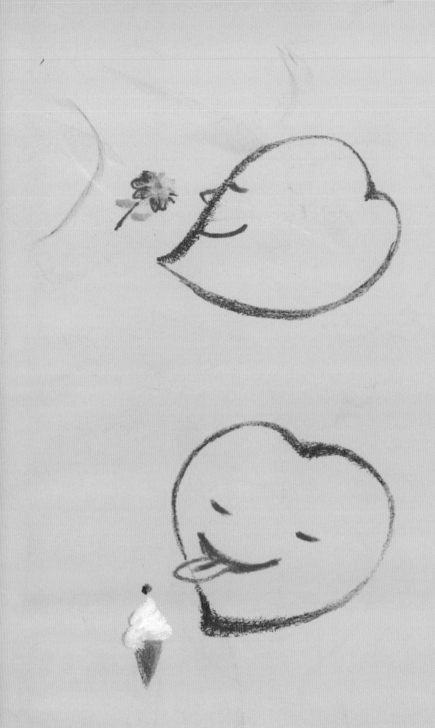

第六個心是意識，也就是我們用來思考、記憶、分析、推理、以及做抽象的思維的心智。此外，意識也能夠分析前五個心所接受的信息。由於意識功能多元，一般人都會把它當成自己的心智。

一般人大概不會知道第七個心是什麼。佛教經典將祂命名為末那識。在這八個心當中，負責做決定的就是末那識，譬如我們決定要睡覺、要出去玩、要吃飯等等，都是末那識在幕後下達指令，我們很難察覺到它的存在。

第八個心叫阿賴耶識，也稱為根本識，或如來藏。祂是最特別最神秘的心；因為祂像一台萬能的錄影機一樣，可以完整無缺地儲存和鉅細靡遺地記錄我們做過的每一件事情。我們平常完全感覺不到祂的存在，但祂卻是我們每個人的生命主體。

換句語說，前六個心接觸和分辨外面世界的形形色色的事物和資訊。第七個心時時裁決、第八個心不偏不倚地記錄並收藏一切。如果我們的身心是一家龐大的公司，這八個心就像八個合作無間、配合得天衣無縫的董事長、總經理、經理、櫃台員工，讓我們可以正常地生活在這個世界上。

在釋迦牟尼佛尚未出現在這個世界之前，沒有人知道每個人都有八個心。不但如此，一般人與大部份的宗教信仰都認為意識就是我們的靈魂；我們死後，祂還能繼續存在，開展下一個階段的生命。

佛陀清楚地告訴我們，意識無法永遠存在。我們睡覺的時候祂就消失了，祂也不能讓自己延續到下一世。真正可以永遠存在的是如來藏，祂會執行因果律———也就是依照我們過去所做的事情，公平客觀地安排我們死後的去處，一點都不會錯亂。做好事的人可以投生到好的地方享樂，做壞事的人必然要承受惡果，例如變成畜生……等。

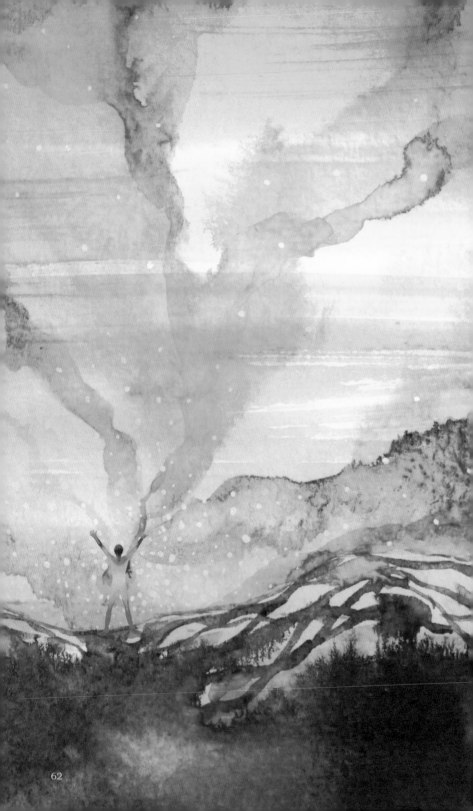

不僅如此，事實上我們每一個人都有一個如來藏。我們的一切，包括我們的身心，都是由自己的如來藏所出生。乃至於每一個生命，即使微小如螞蟻，也有牠自己的如來藏。至於銀河星系、山河大地也是由大家的如來藏共同感應所變現出來的。如來藏是一位名副其實的神奇的無形魔術師。

瞭解人有八個心識到底有何意義？透過認
識這八個心，我們才能夠消除負面的情緒
與習性、提高專注力、獲得正確的認知，
進而活出更健康、幸福、自由、和更有智慧
的豐盛人生。

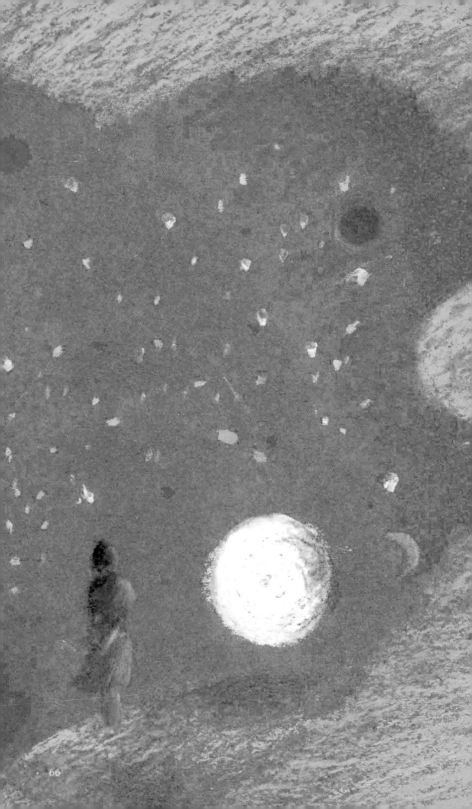

佛陀告訴我們這個生命的秘密，就是希望我們瞭解生命的根源，而能離開一切煩惱與痛苦。當我們找到第八識如來藏，並且全面開發祂所具有的神奇能力，我們就會像佛陀一樣，可以完全掌控自己的生命，得到最終極圓滿的智慧。

所以古人以一首偈語，
來說明我們身中八個心和合運作的道理：
八個兄弟共一胎，一個伶俐一個呆；
五個門前做買賣，一個家裡把帳開。

後記

本書依據玄奘菩薩的著作，向所有讀者介紹佛法所說的八識法義。第八識名為如來藏，又名阿賴耶識、異熟識、無垢識（庵摩羅識），禪宗名之為父母未生前的本來面目、本地風光、無心（無見聞覺知）、真心、金剛心、佛、法、莫邪劍……等。佛教基礎與核心的教義，以及佛弟子證悟的常住真心，都是指這個第八識。

十幾歲就悟得如來藏的玄奘大師，為了求取悟後進修的成佛之道次第與內涵，前往天竺取經，主要是想得到《瑜伽師地論》（又名《十七地論》）。玄奘菩薩停留印度期間，應戒日王之邀，召開了法義辨正無遮大會，大眾信服，名震五印，被天竺外道與佛弟子尊稱為解脫天、大乘第一義天。他深解如來經中說的法義而在回國後翻譯了許多經典，後來接受佛教界的請求而寫了《成唯識論》、《八識規矩頌》，深入解釋這八個識的自性……等，可謂甚深廣大、勝妙無比，至今流傳不歇。

中國佛教史上，玄奘菩薩不是唯一證悟第八識的佛子，禪宗開悟所證同樣也是第八識。禪宗二祖慧可悟得如來藏，菩提達摩以《楞伽經》印證他開悟。六祖慧能悟得如來藏，

五祖弘忍以《金剛經》為他印證開悟時，六祖就說：「何期自性本不生滅、何期自性能生萬法……」。

到了宋朝，弘傳看話禪的大慧宗杲、默照禪的宏智正覺，也都是悟得如來藏而出世弘法，所悟相同所以後來成為莫逆之交。

在西藏地區，篤補巴與多羅那他兩位大師也都證得第八識。證悟如來藏的篤補巴寫了《山法了義海》他空見鉅著，悟得如來藏的多羅那他寫了《他空要義》等重要著作。

相對於不生滅的第八識來說，意識心在眠熟、悶絕、無想定、滅盡定、正死位中都會斷滅，是有生有滅之法，不是從前世來到此世，也不能去到下一世。第六意識要依意根與法塵作助緣，才能從第八識中生起及運作，這是從釋迦牟尼佛以來，古今一切證悟者的現量觀察所知。

靜坐中的離念靈知（包含與五塵同在的離念靈知，以及離五塵的第二禪乃至非想非非想定中的離念靈知），與喇嘛們樂空雙運中不離五塵的離念靈知心，都是意識心。意識依意根與法塵才能從如來藏中生起，意根與法塵也是從看似癡呆的第八識中生起；生起後的意識、意根、法塵，都要在第八識的支援下才能繼續存在及運作。

簡要來說，佛法修行人證悟的心是指第八識，不是意識心。也因此故，凡是不信受佛法經教所說第八識法義，而信受唯有意識存在的人，就永遠無法實證第八識，都無法實證三乘菩提。

正覺各地講堂地址

臺北講堂
地址：台北市大同區承德路三段277號9樓
（台北捷運圓山站旁）電話：(02) 2595-7295
傳真：(02) 2595-4493

大溪正覺祖師堂
地址：大溪鎮美華里信義路650巷坑底5之6號
電話：(03) 388-6110

桃園講堂
地址：桃園市桃園區介壽路286、288號10樓
（陽明運動公園對面）電話：(03) 374-9363

新竹講堂
地址：新竹市東區東光路55號2樓
（合庫銀行2樓隔壁）電話：(03) 572-4297

臺中講堂
地址：台中市南屯區五權西路二段666號13樓之4
（國泰世華銀行13樓）電話：(04) 2381-6090

嘉義講堂
地址：嘉義市西區友愛路288號8樓之1、8樓之2
（彰化銀行8樓）電話：(05) 231-8228

臺南講堂
地址：台南市北區西門路四段15號4樓
（民德國中旁大）電話：(06) 282-0541

高雄講堂
高雄市新興區中正三路45號5樓（復興路與中正路口
捷運信義國小站 旁）電話 (07) 223-4248

美國洛杉磯講堂
地址：825 S. Lemon Ave, Diamond Bar, CA 91798,
U. S. A. 電話：(909) 595-5222；(626) 454-0607

香港講堂
地址：九龍觀塘成業街10號電訊一代廣場27樓E室
電話：(852) 2326-2231

WHOLESOME VISION PUBLICATIONS

1. Signless Buddha-Mindfulness
2. Entering the Dharma-Door of Buddha-Mindfulness
3. Selected Buddhist Writings of the Venerable Xiao Pingshi
4. Behind the Façade of Tibetan Tantra (First Three Parts)
5. The Eight Brothers